Table Of Contents

I0406991

Chapter 1: Introduction to Facebook as a Platform

- The evolution of Facebook: From social network to powerful marketing tool
- Understanding the potential and reach of Facebook's user base
- The role of Facebook in personal and business interactions

Chapter 2: Setting the Foundation

- Creating a personal profile and understanding privacy settings
- Establishing your business presence: Pages vs. Profiles
- Crafting an authentic online persona

Chapter 3: Creating Compelling Content

- The art of storytelling: Engaging your audience with relatable narratives
- Understanding the significance of visual content: Photos, videos, and graphics
- Leveraging the algorithm: Tips for content visibility and engagement

Chapter 4: Building and Growing Your Community

- Identifying your target audience: Demographics, interests, and behaviors
- Strategies for increasing followers and likes
- Encouraging meaningful interactions and fostering a sense of community

Chapter 5: Developing a Content Strategy

- Setting goals: Awareness, engagement, conversions
- Planning a content calendar: Consistency is key
- Balancing promotional and value-driven content

Chapter 6: Engaging Your Audience

- Responding to comments and messages: Timely and thoughtful communication
- Hosting contests, giveaways, and interactive events
- Using Facebook Live and Stories for real-time engagement

Chapter 7: Facebook Advertising Essentials

- Understanding Facebook's advertising options
- Setting up targeted ads: Budgeting, audience segmentation, and ad formats
- Analyzing ad performance and refining strategies

Chapter 8: Utilizing Facebook Groups

- Creating or joining groups aligned with your interests or business
- Nurturing communities within groups: Moderation and value-driven contributions
- Leveraging groups for networking, market research, and feedback

Chapter 9: Measuring Success and Analytics

- Using Facebook Insights to track page performance
- Defining key metrics: Reach, engagement, click-through rates, conversions
- Adapting strategies based on data-driven insights

Chapter 10: Scaling Your Efforts

- Collaborating with influencers and partners
- Expanding to other platforms: Cross-promotion and integration
- Balancing growth with maintaining authenticity and community focus

Chapter 11: Crisis Management and Etiquette

- Addressing negative comments and handling criticism
- Navigating controversial topics while maintaining professionalism
- Adhering to ethical guidelines and best practices

Chapter 12: Evolving Trends and Future Considerations

- Staying updated on Facebook's algorithm changes
- Exploring emerging features: VR, AR, and AI integration
- Diversifying your online presence for long-term success

Conclusion: Your Journey on Facebook

- Reflecting on your progress and accomplishments
- Embracing the ever-changing landscape of social media
- Encouragement to continue learning, adapting, and thriving on Facebook

Remember, success on Facebook requires dedication, creativity, and a genuine desire to connect with your audience. By following the strategies outlined in this book and remaining open to new possibilities, you can build a thriving presence on this influential platform.

Chapter 1

Introduction to Facebook as a Platform

In the world of social media, few platforms have left as indelible a mark as Facebook. What began as a humble college networking site in 2004 has transformed into a global phenomenon that connects billions of people around the world. In this chapter, we'll delve into the evolution of Facebook, its potential as a marketing tool, and the pivotal role it plays in personal and business interactions.

The Evolution of Facebook: From Social Network to Powerful Marketing Tool

Facebook's journey started in a Harvard University dorm room, where Mark Zuckerberg and his co-founders envisioned a digital space for students to connect and share information. As the platform expanded beyond campuses, it quickly gained traction as a social networking site that facilitated connections among friends, family, and acquaintances.

Over time, Facebook evolved from being solely a means of personal communication to a robust platform with various features, including status updates, photo sharing, event planning, and more. The introduction of the "Like" button in 2009 revolutionized how users engaged with content, contributing to the platform's addictive nature.

In recent years, Facebook has transformed into a potent marketing tool. With its expansive user base and sophisticated targeting capabilities, businesses have recognized its potential for reaching specific demographics and engaging potential customers.

Understanding the Potential and Reach of Facebook's User Base

One of Facebook's greatest strengths lies in its colossal user base. As of my last knowledge update in September 2021, Facebook had over 2.8 billion monthly active users, spanning across various demographics, age groups, and regions. This reach presents an incredible opportunity for businesses and individuals to connect with their target audiences.

The diversity of Facebook's user base means that regardless of your niche, industry, or interests, there's likely a community waiting to engage with your content. From stay-at-home parents to tech enthusiasts, from local businesses to international corporations, Facebook's user base offers a vast and potentially receptive audience.

The Role of Facebook in Personal and Business Interactions

Facebook's dual role as a personal and business platform sets it apart from many other social media networks. Individuals use Facebook to connect with friends and family, share life updates, and discover content that aligns with their interests. Meanwhile, businesses leverage Facebook's features to showcase products, provide customer support, and build brand awareness.

For businesses, Facebook offers multiple avenues for interaction:

- **Pages:** Organizations can create dedicated Pages to establish an official online presence. These Pages serve as a hub for sharing updates, responding to inquiries, and building a community around the brand.
- **Groups:** Facebook Groups facilitate more intimate discussions and interactions among like-minded individuals. Businesses can create or participate in Groups relevant to their industry, fostering engagement and trust.
- **Advertising:** With sophisticated advertising tools, businesses can tailor their messages to specific demographics, reaching potential customers based on factors like age, location, interests, and behaviors.

In the digital age, effective online interactions are pivotal for personal connections and business growth. Facebook bridges the gap between these realms, enabling users to engage with both their loved ones and their favorite brands within a single platform.

As you embark on your journey to harness the power of Facebook, remember that understanding its evolution, user base, and dual nature will provide you with a strong foundation for success. In the following chapters, we'll explore the intricacies of creating compelling content, building communities, and utilizing Facebook's advertising capabilities to achieve your goals.

Chapter 2

Setting the Foundation

In the vast landscape of Facebook, establishing a solid foundation is essential to ensuring your success, whether you're an individual seeking personal connections or a business aiming to engage customers. This chapter delves into the key elements of setting the right groundwork: creating a personal profile, navigating privacy settings, establishing a business presence, and crafting an authentic online persona.

Creating a Personal Profile and Understanding Privacy Settings

1. **Create Your Profile:** To begin your journey on Facebook, you'll need to create a personal profile. Fill out your name, add a profile picture, and provide basic information that reflects your identity.

2. **Privacy Settings:** Take control of your online presence by customizing your privacy settings. These settings determine who can see your posts, who can send you friend requests, and what information is publicly accessible. Adjust your settings to align with your comfort level and desired level of visibility.

3. **Posting Privacy:** When you post content on Facebook, you can choose who can see it. Decide whether your posts are public, visible to friends only, or shared with a custom group of people.

Establishing Your Business Presence: Pages vs. Profiles

1. **Pages for Businesses:** If you're representing a business, brand, or organization, it's recommended to create a Facebook Page rather than

using a personal profile. Pages offer business-specific features, analytics, and advertising options.

2. **Benefits of Pages:** Pages allow you to connect with your audience without the limitations of personal profiles. You can access insights about your followers, run targeted ads, and provide customer support. Plus, Pages enable users to engage with your content without requiring mutual friend connections.

3. **Profiles for Individuals:** While Pages are ideal for businesses, individuals should maintain a personal profile. This allows you to connect with friends, family, and acquaintances, and share personal updates.

Crafting an Authentic Online Persona

1. **Consistency and Authenticity:** Authenticity is key to building trust and meaningful connections on Facebook. Ensure that your profile information, posts, and interactions reflect your true personality, values, and interests.

2. **Profile Picture and Cover Photo:** Choose a profile picture that represents you or your brand professionally and is easily recognizable. Your cover photo provides an opportunity to showcase your personality or brand's essence.

3. **Bio and About Section:** Craft a concise yet informative bio that communicates who you are or what your business stands for. Use the "About" section to share additional details, such as contact information and links to your website or other social media profiles.

4. **Engagement and Interaction:** Interact with others in a genuine and respectful manner. Engage with posts, respond to comments, and foster connections that align with your interests or business objectives.

5. **Content Tone and Voice:** Develop a consistent tone and voice for your posts. Whether you're sharing personal updates, industry insights, or promotional content, maintain a style that resonates with your audience.

Remember that your online persona should be an extension of yourself or your brand's identity. Consistency and authenticity build a strong foundation for trust and engagement on Facebook. In the subsequent chapters, we'll explore the art of creating compelling content, growing your community, and refining your strategies for success.

Chapter 3: Creating Compelling Content

In the vast sea of social media, creating content that captivates your audience's attention is the key to success on Facebook. This chapter delves into the art of crafting content that resonates with your followers, the power of visual elements, and strategies for optimizing your content's visibility and engagement through the platform's algorithm.

The Art of Storytelling: Engaging Your Audience with Relatable Narratives

In the digital landscape of Facebook, the art of storytelling holds a remarkable power to captivate your audience's attention and forge lasting connections. This chapter dives deep into the intricacies of storytelling, offering insights into how to craft relatable narratives that resonate with your followers and inspire genuine engagement.

1. Emotion-Fueled Connections

- **Evoke Emotions:** Stories that evoke emotions resonate deeply with your audience. Share personal experiences, challenges overcome, or moments of triumph that your audience can relate to.
- **Empathy and Understanding:** Tap into shared human experiences to foster empathy. When your audience feels understood, they're more likely to engage and connect with your content.

2. Authenticity and Relatability

- **Personal Touch:** Infuse your stories with authenticity by sharing your personal perspectives, struggles, and successes. Transparency builds trust and encourages authenticity in return.

- **Real-Life Examples:** Incorporate real-life examples that your audience can relate to. Showing vulnerability and acknowledging mistakes can create a more authentic connection.

3. Problem-Solution Narratives

- **Identify Challenges:** Highlight challenges that your audience might face. This could be a pain point related to your industry, a common concern, or a relatable struggle.
- **Present Solutions:** After presenting the challenge, offer solutions that align with your expertise. Position your brand or product as a valuable resource that can help address these challenges.

4. Hero's Journey

- **Narrative Arc:** Follow the classic hero's journey narrative structure, where the protagonist faces challenges, undergoes transformation, and emerges stronger. Relate this structure to your brand or message.
- **Your Audience as Heroes:** Position your audience as the heroes of their own stories, with your brand serving as the guide or mentor on their journey.

5. Behind-the-Scenes Glimpses

- **Transparency:** Share behind-the-scenes moments that offer an insider's view of your brand or process. This transparency humanizes your brand and fosters a sense of intimacy.
- **Team Spotlight:** Introduce your team members and their roles. This showcases the people behind your brand and highlights their unique stories.

6. Universal Themes

- **Shared Values:** Connect with your audience through universal themes like family, friendship, personal growth, and resilience. These themes resonate across cultures and backgrounds.

- **Cultural Relevance:** Adapt your storytelling to incorporate cultural references that align with your audience's background, fostering a deeper connection.

Remember that stories are a powerful tool to create emotional resonance, inspire action, and build a loyal community. By infusing your content with relatable narratives, you can establish a genuine connection with your audience, making your brand more memorable and impactful on Facebook. In the forthcoming chapters, we'll explore the significance of visual content and how to leverage the algorithm to maximize your content's visibility and engagement.

Understanding the Significance of Visual Content: Photos, Videos, and Graphics

In the visually-driven world of Facebook, harnessing the power of visual content is essential for capturing your audience's attention and conveying messages effectively. This chapter delves into the significance of visual content, exploring the impact of photos, videos, and graphics, and providing insights into how to use these elements to enhance your presence on the platform.

1. Captivating with Visual Appeal

- **Immediate Impact:** Visual content grabs users' attention faster than text alone. Use striking visuals to stop users in their scrolling tracks.

- **Emotional Resonance:** Images and videos have the ability to evoke emotions, making your content more memorable and relatable.

2. Power of Photos

- **Storytelling Imagery:** Share photos that tell stories on their own. A well-chosen photo can convey emotions, experiences, and messages without the need for extensive text.
- **Product Showcase:** Showcase your products or services through high-quality photos. Highlight key features and benefits to entice your audience.

3. Dynamic Videos

- **Engagement:** Videos tend to generate higher engagement than static content. Create videos that entertain, educate, or inspire your audience.
- **Live Videos:** Use Facebook Live to connect with your audience in real-time. Host Q&A sessions, behind-the-scenes tours, or product launches to engage viewers.

4. Engaging Graphics

- **Infographics:** Simplify complex information by using infographics. Present data, statistics, or step-by-step processes in an easily digestible visual format.
- **Memes and Humor:** Incorporate humor into your graphics, but ensure it aligns with your brand's tone and message. Memes and humorous graphics can resonate with a wide audience.

5. Brand Consistency

- **Visual Identity:** Develop a consistent visual identity that reflects your brand's personality. Consistency helps users recognize your content instantly.
- **Colors and Fonts:** Choose a consistent color palette and font styles for your visuals. These elements contribute to brand recognition.

6. Visual Storytelling

- **Sequential Content:** Use a series of visuals to tell a story. Create a narrative by sharing multiple images or videos that build upon each other.
- **Before and After:** Showcase transformations or progress through before-and-after visuals. This approach is particularly effective for fitness, beauty, and home improvement niches.

7. User-Generated Content

- **Showcasing Your Community:** Share user-generated content that features your products or services. This builds trust and demonstrates customer satisfaction.

- **Contests and Challenges:** Encourage users to create and share their visuals related to your brand. Contests and challenges increase engagement and user involvement.

Visual content is a potent tool for leaving a lasting impression and communicating messages effectively on Facebook. By strategically using photos, videos, and graphics, you can not only engage your audience but also strengthen your brand's identity and impact. In the upcoming chapters, we'll explore how to leverage Facebook's algorithm to maximize the visibility and engagement of your content, along with strategies for building and growing your community.

Leveraging the Algorithm: Tips for Content Visibility and Engagement

Understanding and working with Facebook's algorithm is essential to ensure your content reaches your intended audience and garners the engagement it deserves. This chapter delves into the intricacies of the algorithm and provides valuable tips to maximize your content's visibility and engagement on the platform.

1. Quality Content Takes Priority

- **User-Centric Approach:** The algorithm prioritizes content that users find valuable and engaging. Focus on creating content that resonates with your audience's interests and preferences.
- **Engagement Signals:** Likes, comments, shares, and clicks are key engagement signals. The more users engage with your content, the more the algorithm recognizes its relevance.

2. Consistency is Key

- **Regular Posting:** Consistently sharing content signals to the algorithm that your page is active and relevant. Develop a content calendar to maintain a steady flow of posts.
- **Peak Engagement Times:** Post when your audience is most active to increase the likelihood of immediate engagement.

3. Authentic Engagement

- **Meaningful Interactions:** Prioritize meaningful interactions over superficial engagement. Comments and shares hold more weight than passive likes.
- **Respond to Comments:** Engage with users who comment on your posts. Respond thoughtfully to foster deeper connections.

4. Diversify Content Formats

- **Varied Content Types:** Use a mix of content formats, such as text posts, images, videos, polls, and live videos. Diversity keeps your audience engaged and interested.
- **Native Video Uploads:** Upload videos directly to Facebook rather than sharing links from external platforms. Native videos tend to receive more visibility.

5. Encourage Shares and Comments

- **Engagement Prompts:** Craft content that encourages users to comment or share. Pose questions, polls, or challenges that spark discussions.

- **User-Generated Content:** Request user-generated content and reshare it. User-generated posts often receive more engagement.

6. Go Live and Use Stories

- **Facebook Live:** Host live video sessions to connect with your audience in real time. Live videos tend to receive more interactions.

- **Stories:** Utilize Facebook Stories to provide glimpses into your day-to-day activities. Stories create a sense of immediacy and authenticity.

7. Avoid Engagement Bait

Authenticity Over Baiting:

Avoid using tactics that explicitly ask for likes, shares, or comments. Focus on creating valuable content that naturally elicits engagement.

8. Analyze Insights

Facebook Insights:

Regularly review your page's performance metrics. Understand which posts resonate the most and adjust your content strategy accordingly.

By aligning your content strategy with the algorithm's preferences, you can effectively increase your content's visibility and engagement on Facebook. Remember that the key to success lies in delivering valuable and engaging content that resonates with your audience. In the forthcoming chapters, we'll explore strategies for building and growing your community, as well as crafting a comprehensive content strategy for sustainable success on the platform.

Chapter 4: Building and Growing Your Community: Identifying Your Target Audience

A successful presence on Facebook hinges on your ability to understand and connect with your target audience. In this chapter, we'll delve into the pivotal aspects of identifying your target audience, encompassing demographics, interests, and behaviors. By gaining a comprehensive understanding of your audience, you can tailor your content and engagement strategies to cultivate a vibrant and engaged community.

1. Demographics: Unveiling the Basics

- **Age and Gender:** Pinpoint the age groups and gender distribution of your intended audience. This knowledge shapes the tone and relevance of your content.
- **Location:** Determine the geographic areas where your audience is concentrated. This understanding aids in crafting content that resonates with their regional context.
- **Education and Occupation:** Delve into the educational backgrounds and occupations of your audience. This information informs the depth and style of your content.

2. Interests and Hobbies: Tapping into Passions

- **Specific Interests:** Identify the unique interests and hobbies that capture your audience's attention. Tailor your content to align with these passions.
- **Lifestyle Preferences:** Grasp your audience's lifestyle choices, values, and preferences. Crafting content that mirrors these aspects enhances relatability.

3. Behaviors and Preferences: Navigating Habits

- **Online Behavior:** Analyze how your audience interacts in the digital realm. Understand their online activity patterns, favored platforms, and peak usage times on Facebook.
- **Content Consumption:** Determine the types of content your audience gravitates toward. This insight guides content creation that resonates with their preferences.

4. Pain Points and Needs: Addressing Challenges

- **Identify Pain Points:** Uncover the challenges and issues your audience faces. Develop content that provides solutions and addresses these pain points.
- **Needs and Desires:** Understand the aspirations and desires of your audience. Tailor your content to offer value that aligns with their goals.

5. Engagement Patterns: Fostering Interaction

- **Preferred Content Formats:** Recognize the content formats your audience engages with most enthusiastically. Focus on creating content that matches their preferences.
- **Comments and Shares:** Observe which posts garner the most comments and shares. These insights steer you toward content that sparks conversations.

By diving deep into the demographics, interests, behaviors, and needs of your target audience, you can craft content that resonates on a personal level. This understanding empowers you to create engaging content that forms the bedrock of a thriving community. In the upcoming chapters, we'll explore strategies for increasing followers and likes, as well as nurturing meaningful interactions within your growing community.

Strategies for Increasing Followers and Likes

A growing community on Facebook is a testament to your content's appeal and the value you provide to your audience. In this chapter, we'll delve into effective strategies for increasing your followers and likes, fostering a broader reach, and building a loyal audience that's engaged with your content.

1. Consistent Posting

Regular Updates:

Post consistently to maintain a visible presence on users' feeds. Establish a content calendar to ensure a steady stream of engaging posts.

2. Compelling Content

- **Quality over Quantity:** Prioritize high-quality content that resonates with your target audience. Focus on value, relevance, and entertainment.
- **Diverse Content Formats:** Mix up your content formats with photos, videos, infographics, and text-based posts to cater to different preferences.

3. Utilize Hashtags

Relevant Hashtags:

Incorporate relevant and trending hashtags in your posts. Hashtags improve discoverability and help users find your content.

4. Collaborations and Cross-Promotions

- **Partner with Influencers:** Collaborate with influencers in your niche for shout-outs or joint content. This introduces your content to their followers.
- **Cross-Promotion:** Partner with complementary brands or pages for mutual promotion. This exposes your content to a broader audience.

5. Engage with Your Audience

Respond to Comments:

Engage with users who comment on your posts. Responding shows that you value their interaction and encourages further engagement.

6. Run Contests and Giveaways

- **Engagement Contests:** Host contests that require likes, shares, or comments for entry. This increases engagement and expands your reach.
- **Value-Driven Giveaways:** Offer giveaways that provide value to your audience. This encourages participation and attracts new followers.

7. Facebook Ads

Promoted Posts:

Boost your most engaging posts to reach a wider audience. Use Facebook's ad targeting options to ensure your content reaches the right people.

8. User-Generated Content

Encourage User Participation:

Prompt users to create and share content related to your brand. Repost user-generated content to showcase community involvement.

9. Shareable Content

Content Worth Sharing:

Craft content that users want to share with their networks. This extends your reach organically.

10. Optimize Posting Times

Peak Engagement Hours:

Schedule your posts during peak hours when your target audience is most active on Facebook.

Increasing your followers and likes requires a strategic approach that combines engaging content, thoughtful interactions, and effective promotion. By implementing these strategies, you can gradually build a community of loyal followers who actively engage with your content and contribute to your growth on Facebook. In the next chapter, we'll explore the importance of fostering meaningful interactions and creating a sense of community within your audience.

Encouraging Meaningful Interactions and Fostering a Sense of Community

Creating a thriving community on Facebook goes beyond mere numbers; it's about building genuine connections and fostering a sense of belonging. In this chapter, we'll explore strategies for encouraging meaningful interactions and cultivating a strong sense of community among your followers.

1. Initiate Conversations

- **Thought-Provoking Content:** Share posts that prompt discussions and encourage users to share their opinions, experiences, and insights.
- **Open-Ended Questions:** Pose questions that require more than a simple yes or no answer. Encourage users to elaborate and engage in thoughtful conversations.

2. Respond and Engage

- **Prompt Replies:** Respond promptly to comments on your posts. Acknowledge and engage with your audience's thoughts and queries.
- **Engage with User-Generated Content:** Show appreciation for user-generated content by sharing it and commenting on it. This reinforces a sense of community involvement.

3. Create Polls and Surveys

Crowdsourced Opinions:

Use polls and surveys to involve your audience in decision-making. This gives them a voice and makes them feel invested in your content.

4. Host Live Q&A Sessions

Real-Time Interaction:

Host live video sessions where you answer questions from your audience in real-time. This fosters direct and authentic engagement.

5. Share User Stories

Spotlight User Successes:

Share stories of users who have benefitted from your products or services. Highlighting their achievements creates a sense of camaraderie.

6. Exclusive Content for Followers

Rewards for Engagement:

Offer exclusive content, discounts, or insights to your followers as a reward for their engagement.

7. Facebook Groups

Niche Communities:

Create or participate in Facebook Groups that align with your brand's focus. Groups provide a space for like-minded individuals to connect deeply.

8. Encourage Tagging and Sharing

- **Tagging Friends:** Create posts that encourage users to tag friends who might be interested in the content. This extends your reach organically.
- **Shareable Content:** Craft content that users want to share with their networks. This spreads your message further and widens your community.

9. Acknowledge Milestones

Celebrating Achievements:

Acknowledge and celebrate milestones, both big and small, with your community. This creates a sense of shared accomplishment.

10. Consistency and Authenticity

- **Be Consistent:** Regularly interact and engage with your audience. Consistency builds familiarity and strengthens your community bonds.
- **Authentic Engagement:** Ensure your interactions are genuine and respectful. Authenticity fosters trust and encourages more meaningful connections.

By focusing on meaningful interactions and fostering a sense of community, you create an environment where followers feel valued, connected, and inspired to engage. As you implement these strategies, your Facebook presence will evolve into a space where genuine conversations and connections thrive. In the upcoming chapters, we'll delve into crafting a comprehensive content strategy and effectively utilizing Facebook's advertising options for further growth and impact.

Chapter 5: Developing a Content Strategy

A well-defined content strategy is the backbone of a successful Facebook presence. In this chapter, we'll explore the essential elements of crafting a comprehensive content strategy, including setting goals, planning a content calendar, and striking the right balance between promotional and value-driven content.

1. Setting Goals: Awareness, Engagement, Conversions

- **Awareness:** Define your objectives for increasing brand visibility, reaching a wider audience, and establishing your presence within your niche.
- **Engagement:** Set goals for fostering interactions, encouraging comments, shares, and likes on your content. Engagement boosts visibility and community participation.
- **Conversions:** If applicable, establish goals related to driving specific actions, such as website visits, sign-ups, or purchases.

2. Planning a Content Calendar: Consistency is Key

- **Consistency:** Develop a content calendar that outlines when and what you'll post. Consistency builds anticipation and trust among your audience.
- **Diverse Content:** Include a mix of content formats and topics to cater to various audience preferences.

3. Balancing Promotional and Value-Driven Content

- **Educational Content:** Share informative and valuable content related to your niche. Educating your audience establishes your authority and provides tangible benefits.

- **Entertaining Content:** Craft content that entertains and engages your audience. Humor, stories, and relatable content create a positive user experience.
- **Promotional Content:** Promote your products or services, but avoid overwhelming your audience with constant sales pitches. Maintain a balanced approach.

4. Content Themes and Categories

- **Identify Themes:** Determine overarching themes that align with your brand and resonate with your audience. This helps maintain consistency and relevance.
- **Content Categories:** Organize your content into categories that cover different aspects of your niche. This allows for a well-rounded content mix.

5. Audience Persona Alignment

Tailor Content:

Craft content that aligns with the interests, preferences, and pain points of your audience personas.

6. Storytelling and Personalization

- **Storytelling:** Integrate storytelling into your content to create emotional connections and make your brand more relatable.
- **Personalization:** Address your audience directly and use inclusive language. Personalization enhances engagement and fosters a sense of community.

7. Analyze and Optimize

- **Track Metrics:** Monitor engagement, reach, and conversion metrics to assess the effectiveness of your content strategy.

- **Iterate and Improve:** Use insights from your analytics to refine your content strategy over time. Adapt to changing audience preferences and trends.

By developing a clear and purposeful content strategy, you lay the groundwork for consistent, engaging, and relevant content that resonates with your audience. This strategy forms the backbone of your Facebook presence, enabling you to achieve your goals and create meaningful connections. In the upcoming chapters, we'll explore the world of Facebook advertising and how to leverage it effectively for increased reach and impact.

Chapter 6: Engaging Your Audience

Engaging your audience on Facebook is a vital component of building a vibrant and active community. In this chapter, we'll delve into strategies for effectively engaging your audience, including responding to comments and messages, hosting contests and giveaways, and utilizing Facebook Live and Stories for real-time engagement.

1. Responding to Comments and Messages: Timely and Thoughtful Communication

- **Prompt Replies:** Respond to comments on your posts in a timely manner. This shows your audience that you value their input and encourages further engagement.
- **Private Messages:** Address private messages with the same level of care. Personalized and helpful responses foster positive interactions.

2. Hosting Contests, Giveaways, and Interactive Events

- **Contests:** Organize engaging contests that require user participation. This fosters excitement and encourages users to interact with your content.
- **Giveaways:** Offer valuable prizes through giveaways that motivate users to engage with your posts and share them.
- **Interactive Events:** Host interactive events such as quizzes, polls, or challenges. These activities create opportunities for users to interact with your brand.

3. Using Facebook Live and Stories for Real-Time Engagement

- **Facebook Live:** Host live video sessions where you interact with your audience in real time. Address their questions, share insights, and showcase products or services.

- **Stories:** Utilize Facebook Stories to provide behind-the-scenes glimpses, share updates, and conduct polls in an immediate and engaging format.

4. Encouraging User-Generated Content

- **Contest Entries:** Encourage users to create and share content related to your brand as contest entries. This generates user involvement and diverse content.
- **Sharing Success Stories:** Spotlight user success stories that demonstrate the impact of your products or services. This builds a sense of community and trust.

5. Exclusive Offers for Engaged Users

Rewards for Engagement:

Offer exclusive discounts, early access, or special offers to users who consistently engage with your content.

6. Authentic Interaction

Show Appreciation:

Express gratitude for user comments, shares, and engagement. Authentic interaction fosters a positive relationship with your audience.

7. Consistency in Engagement

Engagement Calendar:

Plan regular engagement activities to keep your audience consistently involved and excited.

8. Monitoring and Analyzing Engagement

- **Track Engagement Metrics:** Monitor likes, comments, shares, and other engagement metrics to understand what resonates with your audience.
- **Iterative Approach:** Adapt your engagement strategies based on the insights gained from analyzing your engagement metrics.

By implementing these strategies, you can create a dynamic and interactive Facebook presence that encourages meaningful connections with your audience. Engaging your audience fosters a sense of community, builds brand loyalty, and increases the visibility of your content. In the upcoming chapters, we'll explore the realm of Facebook advertising and how to leverage it effectively for increased reach and impact.

Chapter 7: Facebook Advertising Essentials

Leveraging Facebook's advertising options is a powerful way to expand your reach and achieve specific goals. In this chapter, we'll delve into the essentials of Facebook advertising, including understanding the available options, setting up targeted ads, and analyzing ad performance for continuous improvement.

1. Understanding Facebook's Advertising Options

- **Boosted Posts:** Amplify the visibility of your posts to a broader audience. This option is ideal for increasing engagement and extending the reach of your content.
- **Facebook Ads Manager:** Create and manage various types of ads with more advanced targeting options and ad formats.
- **Facebook Business Suite:** Utilize this platform to manage your Facebook and Instagram presence, including ads, insights, and engagement, in one place.

2. Setting Up Targeted Ads: Budgeting, Audience Segmentation, and Ad Formats

- **Budget Allocation:** Define your advertising budget and allocate it to specific campaigns. Experiment with different budget levels to optimize results.
- **Audience Segmentation:** Create custom audiences based on demographics, interests, behaviors, and engagement history. This ensures your ads reach the most relevant users.
- **Ad Formats:** Choose from a variety of ad formats such as image ads, video ads, carousel ads, and more. Select formats that best showcase your content and resonate with your audience.

3. Analyzing Ad Performance and Refining Strategies

- **Key Metrics:** Monitor key performance metrics such as click-through rate (CTR), conversion rate, engagement rate, and return on ad spend (ROAS).
- **A/B Testing:** Experiment with different ad variations to determine which elements (such as visuals, copy, or targeting) perform best.
- **Ad Optimization:** Use insights gained from analytics to refine your ad strategies. Adjust targeting, ad content, and budget allocation based on what yields the best results.

4. Scaling Successful Campaigns

- **Incremental Growth:** Gradually increase your budget for successful campaigns to scale your reach while maintaining efficient performance.
- **Expand Audience:** Experiment with expanding your audience segmentation while maintaining relevance to discover untapped potential.

5. Ad Creatives and Copywriting

- **Compelling Visuals:** Use eye-catching images or videos that align with your brand and capture attention.
- **Captivating Copy:** Craft concise and persuasive ad copy that communicates your message effectively.

6. Ad Placement and Scheduling

- **Placement Options:** Choose where your ads appear, including Facebook, Instagram, Audience Network, and Messenger.
- **Scheduling:** Schedule your ads to appear during peak engagement times to maximize visibility and interaction.

7. Retargeting and Lookalike Audiences

- **Retargeting:** Target users who have previously engaged with your content or visited your website. Retargeting reinforces brand awareness and encourages conversions.

- **Lookalike Audiences:** Create audiences similar to your existing customer base. Facebook identifies users with similar traits for targeted ad delivery.

By mastering Facebook's advertising options, you can effectively amplify your brand's visibility and reach on the platform. Analyzing ad performance and refining your strategies based on insights ensures you continuously optimize your campaigns for maximum impact. In the following chapters, we'll explore additional strategies for building and growing your community, as well as ways to measure your overall success on Facebook.

Chapter 8: Utilizing Facebook Groups

Facebook Groups provide a unique opportunity to foster a sense of community and engagement around shared interests or businesses. In this chapter, we'll explore the strategies for effectively utilizing Facebook Groups, including creating or joining groups, nurturing communities within them, and leveraging groups for networking, market research, and feedback.

1. Creating or Joining Groups Aligned with Your Interests or Business

- **Creating Groups:** Establish a dedicated space for your audience to connect, discuss, and engage around a specific interest related to your brand or niche.
- **Joining Groups:** Participate in existing groups that align with your interests or industry. This allows you to engage with a wider audience and contribute your expertise.

2. Nurturing Communities Within Groups: Moderation and Value-Driven Contributions

- **Moderation:** Establish clear rules and guidelines to ensure a positive and respectful environment within the group. Moderate discussions to maintain the quality of interactions.
- **Value-Driven Content:** Share valuable insights, tips, and resources that align with the group's focus. Aim to contribute to meaningful discussions and provide genuine value.

3. Leveraging Groups for Networking, Market Research, and Feedback

- **Networking:** Engage with group members, build relationships, and network with individuals who share similar interests or goals. This can lead to collaborations and partnerships.

- **Market Research:** Use groups as a platform to conduct informal market research. Engage in discussions to understand your audience's pain points, preferences, and needs.
- **Feedback Loop:** Seek feedback on your products, services, or content from group members. Their insights can guide improvements and enhance your offerings.

4. Establishing Your Authority

- **Thought Leadership:** Share your expertise, insights, and valuable information to establish yourself as a knowledgeable authority in your niche.

- **Answer Questions:** Respond to questions and provide solutions within the group to showcase your expertise and willingness to help.

5. Promoting Your Content Strategically

- **Share Relevant Content:** Share your blog posts, videos, or other content that align with the group's interests. Ensure your content provides value and sparks discussions.

- **Promotion vs. Contribution:** Strike a balance between sharing your content and actively contributing to the group's discussions. Avoid excessive self-promotion.

6. Creating Engaging Group Activities

- **Live Sessions:** Host live video sessions within the group to engage directly with members and provide insights or advice.

- **Challenges and Contests:** Organize group challenges, contests, or discussions that encourage active participation and interaction.

7. Building Trust and Loyalty

- **Consistency:** Regularly engage with the group to build familiarity and trust among its members.
- **Authenticity:** Be genuine, transparent, and authentic in your interactions. This helps foster trust and a loyal following.

By effectively utilizing Facebook Groups, you can create a vibrant community around your brand, niche, or interests. Engaging in meaningful discussions, providing value, and nurturing relationships can lead to brand loyalty, partnerships, and valuable insights for your business. In the next chapters, we'll explore measuring your success on Facebook and strategies for long-term growth and sustainability.

Chapter 9

Measuring Success and Analytics

Measuring the effectiveness of your efforts on Facebook is crucial for continuous improvement and achieving your goals. In this chapter, we'll delve into the methods for measuring success using Facebook Insights, defining key metrics, and adapting your strategies based on data-driven insights.

1. Using Facebook Insights to Track Page Performance

- **Facebook Insights:** Utilize this built-in tool to access valuable data about your page's performance, audience engagement, and content reach.

- **Page Summary:** Review an overview of key metrics, such as likes, reach, engagement, and top-performing posts.

2. Defining Key Metrics: Reach, Engagement, Click-Through Rates, Conversions

- **Reach:** Monitor how many users have seen your content. Understand the organic and paid reach to gauge your content's visibility.
- **Engagement:** Track likes, comments, shares, and other forms of interaction with your content. Engagement indicates the resonance of your content.
- **Click-Through Rates (CTR):** Measure the effectiveness of your call-to-action buttons or links in driving users to external websites or landing pages.
- **Conversions:** If applicable, track the actions users take after interacting with your content, such as making purchases or signing up for newsletters.

3. Adapting Strategies Based on Data-Driven Insights

- **Analyze Trends:** Identify patterns and trends in your data. Determine which types of content, posting times, or topics perform best.
- **Identify Top Posts:** Pinpoint your most successful posts in terms of engagement, reach, and conversions. Understand what makes them effective.
- **Refine Content Strategy:** Use insights to refine your content strategy. Focus on creating more of the content that resonates with your audience.
- **Optimize Ad Performance:** Review ad performance metrics to refine your targeting, budget allocation, and ad creatives for better results.

4. Tracking Audience Growth and Demographics

- **Audience Growth:** Monitor the growth rate of your followers over time. Understand which strategies lead to increased page likes.
- **Demographic Insights:** Analyze the demographics of your audience, including age, gender, location, and interests. Tailor your content accordingly.

5. Goal Tracking and ROI

- **Set Clear Goals:** Define specific goals for your Facebook presence, such as brand awareness, engagement, website traffic, or conversions.
- **ROI Calculation:** If applicable, calculate the return on investment (ROI) of your Facebook efforts. Compare the costs of advertising with the outcomes achieved.

6. Regular Assessment and Iteration

- **Regular Check-ins:** Consistently review your performance metrics to track your progress and identify areas for improvement.
- **Iterative Approach:** Continuously adapt your strategies based on insights. Experiment with new ideas while building on what works.

By closely monitoring key metrics, using data to inform your decisions, and adapting your strategies based on insights, you can fine-tune your approach to maximize your success on Facebook. In the next chapters, we'll explore strategies for long-term growth and sustainability, as well as tips for staying up-to-date with evolving trends and changes on the platform.

Chapter 10: Scaling Your Efforts

As your presence on Facebook gains traction, it's essential to explore avenues for scaling your efforts to reach even greater heights. In this chapter, we'll focus on collaborating with influencers and partners as a strategic approach to expanding your reach, enhancing credibility, and achieving new levels of success.

1. Collaborating with Influencers and Partners

- **Identify Relevant Influencers:** Research and identify influencers within your niche who have a substantial following and align with your brand values.
- **Build Relationships:** Reach out to influencers and establish authentic relationships. Engage with their content and demonstrate your genuine interest.
- **Co-Creation of Content:** Collaborate with influencers on content creation, such as guest posts, joint videos, or co-hosted events. This introduces your brand to their audience.
- **Leverage Their Reach:** Benefit from the influencer's reach by exposing your brand to their followers. This can lead to increased visibility and credibility.
- **Authentic Endorsements:** When influencers genuinely endorse your brand, their audience is more likely to trust and engage with your content.
- **Partnerships:** Consider partnering with complementary businesses or brands for mutual promotion. This expands your reach to a broader audience.

2. Leveraging Influencer Marketing

- **Sponsored Posts:** Collaborate with influencers to create sponsored posts that showcase your products or services in an organic and relatable way.

- **Product Reviews:** Invite influencers to review your products or services and share their experiences with their audience.
- **Takeovers and Guest Posts:** Allow influencers to take over your account for a day or contribute guest posts. This brings their unique perspective to your audience.

3. Measuring Influencer Campaign Success

- **Set Clear Goals:** Define specific goals for your influencer campaigns, such as increased brand awareness, engagement, or website traffic.
- **Track Key Metrics:** Monitor metrics such as engagement rate, reach, click-through rate, and conversions driven by the influencer's content.
- **ROI Calculation:** Evaluate the return on investment by comparing the costs of the influencer collaboration with the outcomes achieved.

4. Building Authentic Partnerships

- **Shared Values:** Choose influencers and partners who align with your brand's values, ensuring an authentic and meaningful collaboration.
- **Long-Term Relationships:** Focus on building long-term relationships with influencers and partners for consistent and sustained results.

5. Compliance and Transparency

- **Disclosure:** Ensure that influencers clearly disclose any paid partnerships or sponsorships as per legal requirements and ethical practices.
- **Transparency:** Maintain open communication with influencers and partners throughout the collaboration process.

By effectively collaborating with influencers and partners, you can tap into their established audiences and benefit from their credibility and expertise. These collaborations can amplify your reach, enhance your brand's image, and contribute to your overall growth on Facebook. In the upcoming chapters, we'll explore ways to stay updated with platform changes and emerging trends, ensuring your strategies remain relevant and effective.

Expanding to Other Platforms: Cross-Promotion and Integration

While Facebook offers a powerful platform, expanding your presence to other platforms can further amplify your reach and diversify your audience. In this chapter, we'll explore strategies for cross-promotion and integration across different platforms, allowing you to create a cohesive online presence.

1. Cross-Promotion: Leveraging Your Existing Audience

- **Promote Other Platforms:** Encourage your Facebook audience to connect with you on other social media platforms, such as Instagram, Twitter, LinkedIn, or YouTube.
- **Highlight Exclusive Content:** Tease exclusive content available on other platforms to entice your Facebook followers to explore your presence elsewhere.
- **Collaborate Across Platforms:** Partner with influencers or brands for cross-platform collaborations that introduce you to new audiences.

2. Consistent Branding and Messaging

- **Unified Branding:** Maintain consistent branding elements, such as profile pictures, banners, and color schemes, across all platforms.
- **Unified Messaging:** Ensure your core messaging and values are consistent regardless of the platform. This reinforces your brand identity.

3. Integrating Content Strategy

- **Repurpose Content:** Adapt and repurpose your Facebook content for other platforms. Tailor the format to match each platform's strengths and audience preferences.

- **Platform-Specific Content:** Create content that caters to the unique features and audience expectations of each platform.

Balancing Growth with Authenticity and Community Focus

Maintaining authenticity and community focus is essential as you strive for growth on Facebook and other platforms. In this chapter, we'll explore strategies for striking a balance between scaling your efforts and preserving the genuine connections you've established.

1. Value-Driven Growth

- **Prioritize Value:** As you expand, continue delivering value to your audience. Put their needs and interests at the forefront of your efforts.
- **Quality over Quantity:** Focus on creating meaningful interactions rather than solely pursuing large numbers of followers.

2. Consistent Engagement

- **Maintain Engagement:** As your audience grows, continue engaging with your followers on a personal level. Respond to comments and messages authentically.
- **Community Involvement:** Keep your community engaged by hosting interactive events, Q&A sessions, and contests that encourage participation.

3. Humanize Your Brand

- **Share Behind-the-Scenes Content:** Offer glimpses into your daily work, team members, and the human side of your brand. This fosters relatability and connection.
- **Personal Interaction:** Interact with your audience as a person, not just a brand. Share personal stories and experiences to build emotional connections.

4. Regular Self-Assessment

- **Stay True to Values:** Continuously evaluate your actions and strategies to ensure they align with your brand's values and mission.
- **Listen to Feedback:** Pay attention to feedback from your audience. Adapting based on their input maintains community involvement.

5. Empower Your Community

- **User-Generated Content:** Encourage your community to create and share content related to your brand. Highlighting their contributions fosters a sense of ownership.
- **Feedback Channels:** Provide avenues for your audience to share feedback, suggestions, and ideas. Involve them in shaping your growth strategies.

6. Embrace Evolution

Adapt to Change:

Embrace change while maintaining your core values. As you expand and evolve, ensure your brand's identity remains consistent.

Balancing growth with authenticity and community focus is a delicate process that requires continuous effort. By prioritizing meaningful connections and genuine interactions, you can sustain your community's loyalty and engagement while expanding your presence across various platforms. In the upcoming chapters, we'll explore ways to stay updated with platform changes and emerging trends, ensuring your strategies remain relevant and effective.

Chapter 11: Crisis Management and Etiquette

Maintaining a positive online reputation and handling challenging situations with grace is essential for long-term success on Facebook and other platforms. In this chapter, we'll explore strategies for crisis management and maintaining proper etiquette, including addressing negative comments, handling criticism, navigating controversial topics, and adhering to ethical guidelines.

1. Addressing Negative Comments and Handling Criticism

- **Stay Calm:** Respond to negative comments with a composed and respectful tone. Avoid getting defensive or confrontational.
- **Acknowledge Concerns:** Address the concerns raised in the comment while maintaining a solution-oriented approach.
- **Move to Private Channels:** If appropriate, offer to continue the conversation privately to resolve the issue more effectively.

2. Navigating Controversial Topics While Maintaining Professionalism

- **Stay Neutral:** If possible, refrain from taking a strong stance on polarizing topics that may alienate part of your audience.
- **Foster Constructive Discussions:** Encourage open and respectful discussions on controversial topics while moderating to prevent disrespectful behavior.
- **Focus on Relevance:** Share content related to your niche and industry. Avoid straying too far from your expertise into unrelated contentious issues.

3. Adhering to Ethical Guidelines and Best Practices

- **Transparency:** Be transparent about your affiliations, sponsorships, and partnerships. Honesty builds trust with your audience.
- **Respect Privacy:** Protect user privacy and refrain from sharing sensitive information without consent.

- **Avoid Misinformation:** Verify information before sharing it. Sharing inaccurate information damages your credibility.

4. Swift and Thoughtful Responses

- **Timely Responses:** Address comments, messages, and inquiries promptly to demonstrate your commitment to engagement.
- **Thoughtful Responses:** Take the time to craft thoughtful and well-considered responses, even in challenging situations.

5. Draft Crisis Management Plan

- **Preparation:** Develop a crisis management plan outlining how to address various negative scenarios effectively.
- **Internal Communication:** Ensure your team is aligned on the plan and can execute it seamlessly.

6. Professional Tone and Language

- **Maintain Professionalism:** Use a professional and respectful tone in all interactions, even when faced with negativity.
- **Avoid Arguments:** Refrain from engaging in arguments or heated discussions. Focus on constructive dialogue.

7. Learn from Feedback

- **Constructive Feedback:** Embrace feedback, even if it's critical. Use it as an opportunity to improve your strategies and offerings.
- **Apologize When Necessary:** If you make a mistake, apologize sincerely and address the issue promptly.

By mastering crisis management and adhering to proper etiquette, you can build a reputation for professionalism and empathy. Responding to challenges with grace and addressing negative situations effectively will strengthen your brand's credibility and maintain a positive online presence. In the final chapters, we'll explore staying updated with platform changes and trends and creating a lasting impact on Facebook and beyond.

Chapter 12: Evolving Trends and Future Considerations

To remain competitive and successful on Facebook and other platforms, it's crucial to stay updated on the latest trends and emerging features. In this final chapter, we'll explore strategies for staying informed about algorithm changes, embracing emerging technologies like virtual reality (VR), augmented reality (AR), and artificial intelligence (AI) integration, and diversifying your online presence for long-term success.

1. Staying Updated on Facebook's Algorithm Changes

- **Follow Official Channels:** Stay informed by following official Facebook blogs, news updates, and announcements about algorithm changes.
- **Engage in Community:** Participate in online communities, groups, or forums where professionals discuss and analyze algorithm updates.
- **Adapt and Experiment:** Be prepared to adjust your strategies based on algorithm changes. Experiment to identify new approaches that align with updated algorithms.

2. Exploring Emerging Features: VR, AR, and AI Integration

- **Virtual Reality (VR):** Investigate opportunities to incorporate VR content, such as immersive experiences, virtual tours, or product demonstrations.
- **Augmented Reality (AR):** Consider using AR features to allow users to interact with your products or visualize how they fit into their lives.
- **Artificial Intelligence (AI) Integration:** Explore AI-driven chatbots for customer support, personalized recommendations, and predictive analytics.

3. Diversifying Your Online Presence for Long-Term Success

- **Multi-Platform Presence:** Don't rely solely on Facebook. Diversify your presence across various platforms that cater to your target audience.
- **Content Adaptation:** Tailor your content to each platform's strengths and audience preferences while maintaining a consistent brand message.
- **Website and Blog:** Invest in a website and blog to establish a central hub for your online presence, where you have full control over content and branding.

4. Long-Term Brand Building

- **Consistent Branding:** Maintain consistent branding across all platforms to reinforce your identity and foster recognition.
- **Adapt and Innovate:** Embrace change and innovation while remaining true to your brand values and core mission.

Conclusion: Your Journey on Facebook

Congratulations on completing this comprehensive guide to starting, growing, and succeeding on Facebook! You've embarked on a journey that has equipped you with valuable insights, strategies, and tools to navigate the dynamic world of social media marketing. As you reflect on your progress and accomplishments, remember that success on Facebook is not just about numbers but also about the meaningful connections you've forged and the impact you've made.

In the ever-changing landscape of social media, embracing change and innovation is key. The strategies you've learned here have provided a solid foundation, but staying up-to-date with emerging trends and adapting to new challenges is crucial for sustained success.

As you move forward, here's some encouragement to guide you on your continued journey:

1. Continuous Learning and Adaptation

Keep learning and staying curious about the latest developments in social media marketing. The digital landscape evolves rapidly, and your willingness to adapt will set you apart.

2. Authenticity and Value

Always prioritize delivering value to your audience and building authentic relationships. This approach will help you foster a dedicated community that trusts and engages with your brand.

3. Balancing Growth and Community Focus

As you scale your efforts, remember to maintain the sense of community and personal engagement that you've cultivated. It's these connections that will truly set you apart.

4. Embracing Change

Don't fear change; embrace it. The world of social media is dynamic, and those who adapt and innovate will continue to thrive.

5. Building Long-Term Brand Equity

Your success on Facebook is a journey, not a destination. Focus on building a strong brand that resonates with your audience and stands the test of time.

6. Collaboration and Networking

Don't hesitate to collaborate with others and learn from fellow professionals. Networking can lead to new opportunities and insights.

7. Setting Meaningful Goals

Define your goals based on what truly matters to your brand and audience. Meaningful objectives will guide your strategies and actions effectively.

Your journey on Facebook is a testament to your dedication, creativity, and perseverance. As you continue to learn, adapt, and thrive, remember that the skills and knowledge you've gained here will serve as valuable assets in your pursuit of digital success. Keep exploring, experimenting, and making a positive impact on the platform and beyond. Best of luck on your journey of growth and success!

- **Introduction to Facebook as a Platform**
  - o **Understand Facebook's evolution and potential.**
  - o Recognize the role of Facebook in personal and business interactions.
- **Setting the Foundation**
  - o **Create a personal profile and adjust privacy settings.**
  - o **Establish a business presence using Pages.**
  - o **Craft an authentic online persona.**
- **Creating Compelling Content**
  - o Master the art of storytelling to engage your audience.
  - o Recognize the significance of visual content (photos, videos, graphics).
  - o Leverage the algorithm for content visibility and engagement.
- **Building and Growing Your Community**
  - o Identify your target audience's demographics, interests, behaviors.
  - o Implement strategies for increasing followers and likes.
  - o Encourage meaningful interactions and community building.
- **Developing a Content Strategy**
  - o Set clear goals for awareness, engagement, and conversions.
  - o Plan a consistent content calendar.

- o   Balance promotional and value-driven content.
- **Engaging Your Audience**
  - o   Respond to comments and messages promptly.
  - o   Host contests, giveaways, and interactive events.
  - o   Use Facebook Live and Stories for real-time engagement.
- **Facebook Advertising Essentials**
  - o   Understand Facebook's advertising options.
  - o   Set up targeted ads (budgeting, audience segmentation, ad formats).
  - o   Analyze ad performance and refine strategies.
- **Utilizing Facebook Groups**
  - o   Create/join groups aligned with your interests/business.
  - o   Nurture communities within groups (moderation, value-driven contributions).
  - o   Leverage groups for networking, research, and feedback.

- **Measuring Success and Analytics**
  - o   Use Facebook Insights to track page performance.
  - o   Define key metrics (reach, engagement, CTR, conversions).
  - o   Adapt strategies based on data-driven insights.
- **Scaling Your Efforts**
  - o   Collaborate with influencers and partners.
  - o   Maintain authenticity and community focus while growing.
- **Crisis Management and Etiquette**
  - o   Address negative comments and handle criticism professionally.
  - o   Navigate controversial topics while maintaining professionalism.
  - o   Adhere to ethical guidelines and best practices.
- **Evolving Trends and Future Considerations**
  - o   Stay updated on Facebook's algorithm changes.
  - o   Explore emerging features (VR, AR, AI integration).
  - o   Diversify your online presence for long-term success.
- **Conclusion: Your Journey on Facebook**
  - o   Reflect on progress and accomplishments.
  - o   Embrace change in the social media landscape.

       ○   Continue learning, adapting, and thriving.

1. **Engaging Question Post:**

   "Our recent survey revealed that 80% of people prefer outdoor activities. What's your favorite outdoor adventure?"

2. **Educational Post:**

   "Did you know? Studies show that getting 7-9 hours of sleep can boost productivity by 20%. Prioritize your rest!"

3. **Customer Testimonial Post:**

   "Check out this amazing transformation! [Customer Name] lost 15 pounds with our fitness program. Join the journey!"

4. **Tips and Tricks Post:**

   "According to research, drinking 8 glasses of water a day can improve skin hydration by 25%. Stay hydrated for that glow!"

5. **Inspirational Quote Post:**

   "Studies reveal that a positive mindset can increase overall happiness by 30%. Keep focusing on the bright side."

6. **Promotional Post:**

   "Data shows that our [Product] has a satisfaction rate of 95%. Grab yours now and experience the difference!"

7. **Behind-the-Scenes Post:**

   "Curious about our production process? Our latest data-driven video shows the meticulous steps behind our craftsmanship."

8. **Announcement Post:**

   "Exciting news! Our recent poll indicates that 70% of you want a new [Feature]. Guess what? It's coming soon!"

1. **Call-to-Action Post:**

   "Join the webinar that 90% of attendees found beneficial. Learn [Topic] from experts on [Date]. Reserve your spot!"

2. **Engagement Post:**

   "According to our recent poll, [Favorite Book Genre] is the most popular among our community. Share your top pick!"

Remember to incorporate relevant and accurate data into your posts to provide valuable insights to your audience. This can help enhance your credibility and engagement on the platform.

www.ingramcontent.com/pod-product-compliance
Lightning Source LLC
Chambersburg PA
CBHW062254290526
45794CB00006B/2547